Science Technology Engineering Math

STEM STARTERS FOR KIDS

METEOROLOGY

ACTIVITY

Book

PACKED WITH ACTIVITIES AND METEOROLOGY FACTS

Written by Jenny Jacoby

Designed and illustrated by Vicky Barker

Racehorse for
Young Readers

Racehorse for Young Readers books may be purchased in bulk at special discounts for sales promotions, corporate gifts, fund-raising or education purposes. Special editions can also be created to specifications. For details, contact the Special Sales Department at Skyhorse Publishing, 307 West 36th Street, 11th Floor, New York, NY 10018 or info@ skyhorsepublishing.com.

Racehorse for Young Readers is a pending trademark of Skyhorse Publishing, Inc.®, a Delaware corporation.

Visit our website at skyhorsepublishing.com

10 9 8 7

Production by Madeleine Ehm

Printed in China

ISBN 978-1-63158-428-2

WHAT IS METEOROLOGY?

Meteorology is the study of the weather. We all study the weather each day when we step outside and wonder if it will be rainy or chilly or hot. Meteorologists study weather patterns to understand and predict the weather. With climate change creating increasingly unusual weather, there is a lot for meteorologists to study!

WHAT IS STEM?

STEM stands for "science, technology, engineering, and mathematics." These four areas are closely linked, and each of them is important to meteorology. Observing the weather is a science that uses engineering and technology such as satellites to measure the weather, and math to understand weather patterns and make predictions about what the weather will be like.

Science   Technology   Engineering   Math

MEASURING WEATHER

The first step in studying the weather is to observe what the weather is doing in your area. Here are some of the tools meteorologists use.

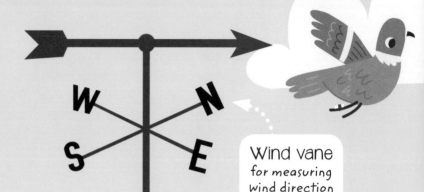

Wind vane
for measuring wind direction

Barometer
for measuring atmospheric pressure (in high pressure, skies are clear; in low pressure, clouds are likely)

Anemometer
for measuring wind speed

Hygrometer
for measuring humidity (how much water is in the air)

Thermometer
for reading temperature

Notepad and pen
for recording readings

Rain gauge
for measuring rainfall

WINDY DAYS

Tools for measuring the wind sit at 33 feet above the ground. Anemometers measure the wind speed by counting how fast the cups spin around, and a weather vane spins around to show the direction the wind is coming from.

Can you tell where the wind is coming from in each of these pictures? Draw an arrow to show the direction the wind is blowing.

WHAT MAKES IT RAIN?

Rain and making clouds are part of the water cycle.

As the water vapor gets higher in the sky it cools down, which condenses it into clouds.

When the clouds get full of water and heavy enough, rain falls (or snow, if it's cold enough).

Water from the land, rivers, ponds, lakes, and seas is warmed by the sun and evaporates into the air.

Rainwater runs over the land and collects in lakes, streams, or rivers and returns to the sea.

Complete this picture by adding your own drawings
of the following items that rely on the water cycle:

- a boat on the water
- a group of fish
- trees enjoying the rain
- a glass of water for each person at the picnic
- an umbrella for someone caught in the rain
- a fishing rod for the boy wanting to fish

CLOUD SPOTTING

There are three main types of cloud and their names are all Latin words that describe how they look.

cloud type	description	Latin meaning
Cumulus	These look like cotton balls	heap
Stratus	Flat, grey sheets of cloud	flattened
Cirrus	Wispy clouds that look like horse tails	lock or tuft of hair

These three main cloud types combine with each other to describe different types of cloud. And if the cloud is a rain cloud it is given another new name: **nimbus.** What does each cloud type do?

Cirrostratus
Can indicate what the weather will be like for the next 24 hours—if it's in a layer that covers the sky there will likely be persistent rain. If it's wispy like animal fur, there will only be light drizzle.

Cirrus
Usually a sign that the weather will change.

Cirrocumulus
Appear with fair weather but often come before stormy weather.

Stratus
Usually don't produce rain—or light drizzle. Low stratus clouds are misty fog.

Cumulus
Most common type of cloud—usually form on sunny days but can cause rain or snow.

Nimbostratus
Continuous rain or snow, lasting for several hours.

Stratocumulus
Often present whatever the weather—and don't create rain.

Cumulonimbus
Heavy rainfall, hail storms, and lightning.

Use the key to draw the clouds and the type of weather expected from each of these cloud types. Will you have to bring an umbrella?

Stratus

Cumulonimbus

Cirrus

Cirrocumulus

RAINBOWS

Rainbows are weather at its most colorful, but they only happen when the conditions are just right. To see a rainbow, you must be facing rain with the sun shining behind you.

How do rainbows work?

You can't touch a rainbow, only see it. That's because rainbows are a trick of the light. Pure light is actually made up of all of the colors of the rainbow. When light gets split up into all of its separate colors we get to see a rainbow. Fine rain and water mist are really good at splitting light up into all of its colors, which is why we see a rainbow when the sun is shining at the rain.

Did you know?

The size of the rainbow depends on how high the sun is in the sky. When the sun is very high you'll only be able to see part of the rainbow. The lower in the sky the sun gets, the more of the rainbow arc you can see.

Conditions are just right for a rainbow! Use markers or colored pencils to draw a rainbow.

Red, Orange, Yellow, Green, Blue, Indigo, Violet

WHAT MAKES IT SNOW?

Snow forms when there is enough moisture in the air and when the air temperature is below freezing (32° Fahrenheit). In other words, it's the same as when rain clouds form except that it's so cold that instead of forming raindrops, the water turns to ice crystals. When enough ice crystals gather together, the snow cloud becomes heavy and snow falls.

As the snow falls, the air temperature determines the sort of snow that falls. If the air is below freezing, the snow falls as tiny flakes, which make powdery snow that is good for skiing.

If the air is slightly above freezing (32–36° Fahrenheit), the flakes will melt slightly and clump together into big fluffy flakes, which make the right kind of snow for making snowmen.

If the air is warmer than 36° Fahrenheit, the snow will melt on its way down and fall as sleet or rain.

In these snowy scenes draw a snowman, a skier, or an umbrella to match the temperature shown.

- less than 32° Fahrenheit: good for skiing
- 32-36° Fahrenheit: good for snowmen
- more than 36° Fahrenheit: bring an umbrella!

37°
Fahrenheit

30°
Fahrenheit

34°
Fahrenheit

TEMPERATURE

There are lots of different reasons for how hot or cold it is where you are today. The temperature depends on:

How far from the equator you are

This is called **latitude.** The closer to the equator, the hotter the temperature can get.

The season

In summer, it's warmer because the land faces the warm sun, but it's cooler in winter because the land faces away from the sun.

How high above sea level you are

This is called **altitude.** Being up a mountain is cooler than being on ground level.

North

Northern Hemisphere

Equator

Southern Hemisphere

South

If you are facing north or south

In the Northern Hemisphere, south-facing hills get more warming sunshine than north-facing slopes. In the Southern Hemisphere, north-facing slopes get more sunshine.

Wind

Wind makes the air feel cooler.

How far from the sea you are

The sea cools and warms more slowly than the land, so temperatures get both hotter and colder the further inland you go.

This map of the world shows the average temperature over December, January, and February. This is summer time in the Southern hemisphere and winter in the Northern hemisphere. Use the temperature key to color in each area. Do the temperatures match the rules?

Rotate me!

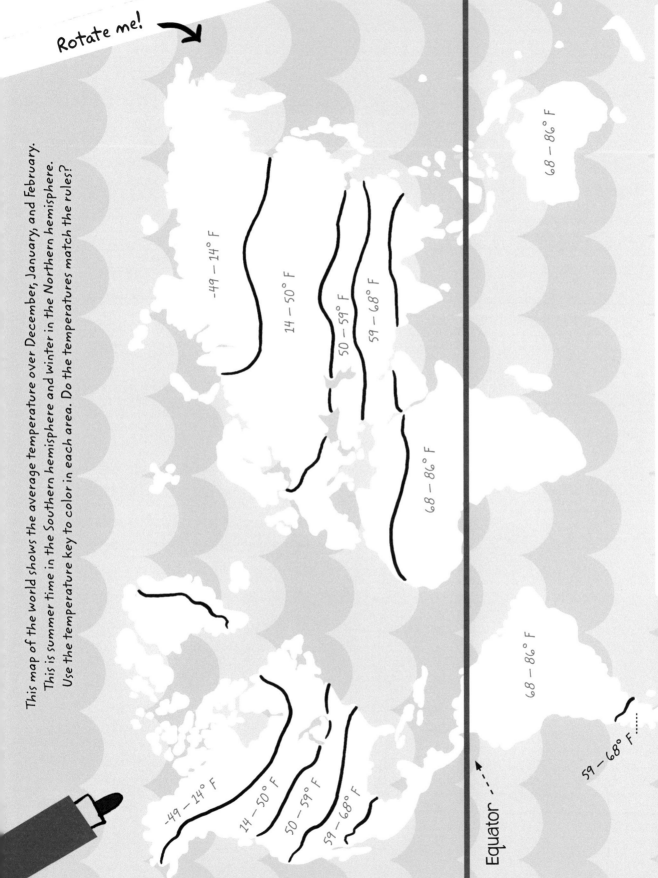

-49 – 14° F

14 – 50° F

50 – 59° F

59 – 68° F

68 – 86° F

68 – 86° F

-49 – 14° F

14 – 50° F

50 – 59° F

59 – 68° F

68 – 86° F

59 – 68° F

Equator

90
80
70
60
50
40
30°F
20
10
0
-10
-20
-30
-40
-50
-60

THUNDER AND LIGHTNING

Lightning happens when the tiny ice crystals inside a big cloud move around inside the cloud, bumping into each other. As they rub together they build up electric charge. When enough charge has built up, the electrical force connects with the electrical charges on the ground, creating a lightning strike.

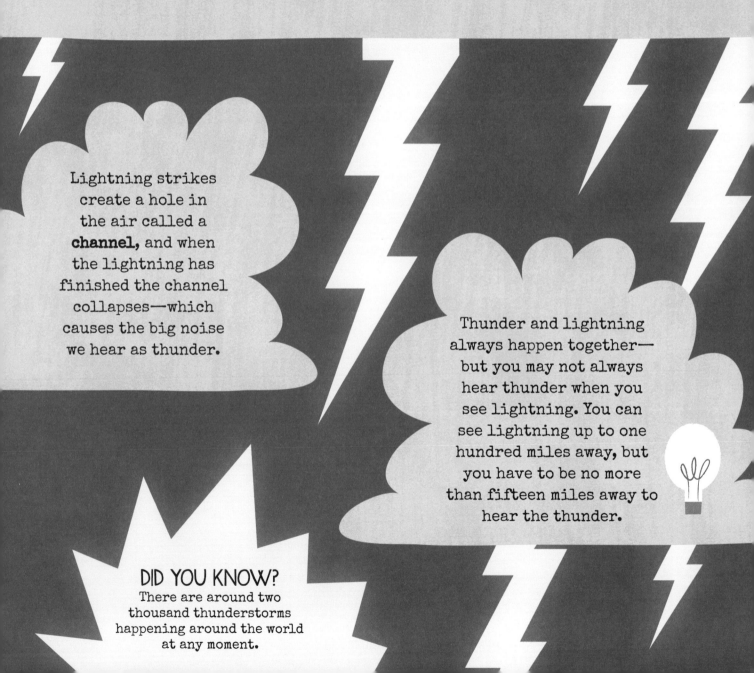

Lightning strikes create a hole in the air called a **channel,** and when the lightning has finished the channel collapses—which causes the big noise we hear as thunder.

Thunder and lightning always happen together— but you may not always hear thunder when you see lightning. You can see lightning up to one hundred miles away, but you have to be no more than fifteen miles away to hear the thunder.

DID YOU KNOW?
There are around two thousand thunderstorms happening around the world at any moment.

It's very
stormy over this country!
Help the airplane to find a safe path
through the storm clouds.

FINISH

TORNADOES

Tornadoes are spinning columns of air that are the most violent effect of powerful thunderstorms. They can travel at more than 250 miles per hour, sucking up objects from the the ground and swirling them upwards in the wind. They can cause a lot of damage to built-up towns and cities.

Tornadoes only happen when moist, warm, low-level winds meet cold, higher-level winds. This clash creates groups of thunder clouds called **supercells,** which have swirling columns of wind within the huge clouds. If a cold wind brings one of the windy swirls down from the cloud to the ground, it is a tornado.

MONSOON

Tropical parts of the world have two main seasons: dry and monsoon. The change from one season to the other can be very dramatic. In some places the monsoon season brings up to 90 percent of the year's rainfall. Perhaps the seasons should be called very dry and very wet! The problem with a lot of rain all at once is flooding, because land that has been dry for several months isn't able to deal with it all at once.

In monsoon time it's very wet but also still hot. Circle the items that would be useful during monsoon.

CHANGING THE WEATHER

Wouldn't it be good if we could make it rain over places that are too dry? Or stop a hurricane from destroying buildings? Scientists are investigating ways to modify the weather to make our lives safer.

Not all scientists agree that "cloud seeding" technology works, but some hot countries with limited water use this clever idea to encourage it to rain.

Water is heated by the sun and turns to vapor in the air.

Water vapor rises and cools high up in the sky to turn into clouds. In some hot, dry countries, there isn't enough water vapor to group together into a cloud.

When the clouds are heavy enough with water, it rains.

Airplanes fly up to scatter substances that encourage water vapor to form into clouds that will rain.

This airplane is drawing a picture in the sky with the clouds it is seeding. Use colored pencils to trace the plane's path and reveal the picture.

CLIMATE CHANGE

Weather changes. Some winters are colder than others—these differences each year are normal. The climate has always changed over longer times too—in the Ice Age, much of Europe was covered in ice; there was a warmer period in the Middle Ages, then a "little ice age" that lasted from about 1300 to 1850 AD.

Since humans started burning fossil fuels (such as coal and oil), the climate has changed at a faster rate. Pollution from these fuels creates **greenhouse gases,** which act like a warm coat around the Earth, making it warmer overall. Glaciers and ice sheets are shrinking, making sea levels rise.

It's not just the temperature that's changing. Some parts of the world are getting dryer, some wetter, and everywhere is seeing unusual weather.

Raining frogs

Flooding

True or false?
Which of these phenomena are likely to be the result of climate change in the future? Check your answers on page 32.

WEIRD WEATHER

Even normal weather can be surprising—so imagine finding it's raining frogs, or even red rain! This weird weather has really happened. But as amazing as it is, it's actually simple: if something can get sucked up with the wind, it can be carried many hundreds of miles before it is dropped again as "rain." So, if a tornado passes over water it could pick up lots of frogs or fish, for example, which can be carried a long way from home before raining back down to earth. If winds pick up lots of red dust from somewhere dry and dusty, it can be carried in the high winds and mix with water vapor in clouds, turning the rain red.

This tornado has picked up a lot of red dust from the desert. Follow the path of the wind to find out where the weird red rain will end up. Avoid the obstacles!

GREECE

EGYPT

SRI LANKA

29

ANSWERS

page 4-5

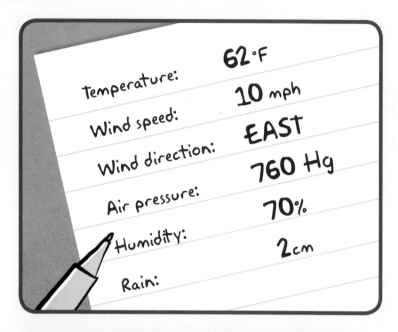

temperature:	62 °F
Wind speed:	10 mph
Wind direction:	EAST
Air pressure:	760 Hg
Humidity:	70%
Rain:	2 cm

page 6-7

page 14-15

page 10-11

Stratus **(foggy)**
Cumulonimbus **(heavy rain)**
Cirrus **(fair, maybe breezy)**
Cirrocumulus **(fair weather)**

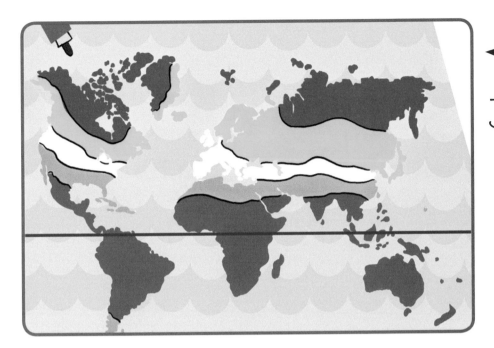

page 16-17

page 18-19

FINISH

page 20-21

There are **18** tornadoes on the map.

page 22-23

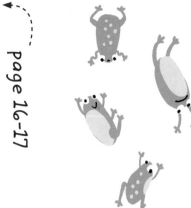

page 24-25

page 26-27

False
- Raining frogs
- Ice skating on downtown rivers
- More earthquakes

True
- More frequent heatwaves
- Flooding
- Stronger, more damaging tropical storms
- Loss of coral reefs
- More forest fires

Page 28-29